MAKING PUPPETS

Josie McKinnon

MAGIC BEAN
IN - FACT

Contents

Introduction

This book describes how to make different types of puppets. These puppets are made from many different materials. The materials you use will depend upon the puppet that you wish to make.

Collecting interesting materials for puppet making can be fun. You can store them in your own puppet-making box. Make sure you gather all the materials needed before you begin to make a puppet.

Anything can be used to make puppets — just use your imagination.

Paper finger puppets

What you need:

- thin, stiff cardboard (approx. 10 cm x 15 cm)
- paint, felt pens, crayons
- collage materials (wool, buttons, paper)
- scissors
- glue
- ruler

Instructions:

1. Photocopy the pattern provided on page 31. Glue the photocopy onto the cardboard.

2. Cut out the shape.

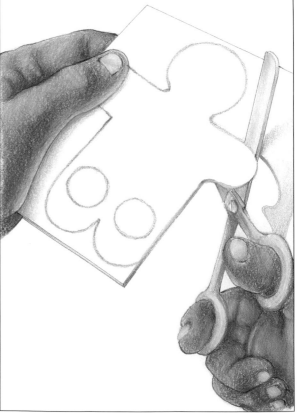

3. Cut out the two finger holes.

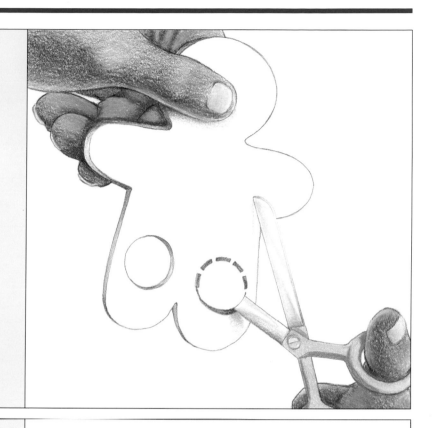

4. Decorate the puppet using paint, felt pens or crayons and collage materials.

5. Push two fingers through the holes to make the puppet walk.

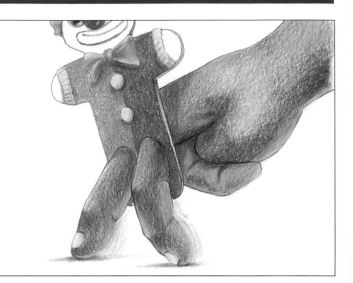

Variations

You can use any drawing or shape.

Attach paper loops to the back of the puppet instead of finger holes.

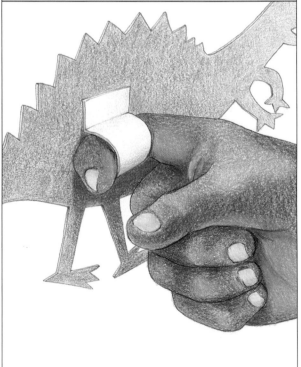

Felt finger puppets

What you need:

- piece of felt
  (approx. 14 cm x 8 cm)
- sewing needle
- cotton thread
- collage materials
  (wool, buttons, sequins)
- scissors
- glue
- felt pens

Instructions:

1. Fold the piece of felt in half.

2. Place your finger on the felt and draw a line around it.

3. Draw another line 2 cm from the first line. Try to keep the same shape. This will be the cutting line.

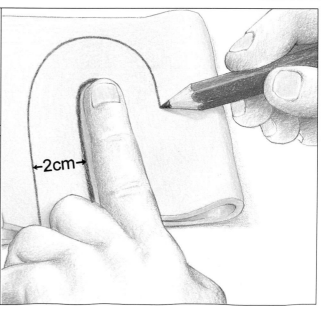

←2cm→

4. Cut out the two layers of fabric.

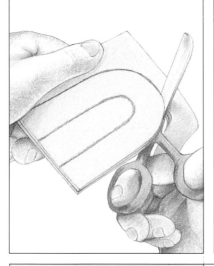

5. Sew the two pieces together. Leave the base edge free for your finger.

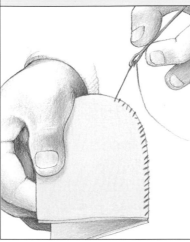

6. Turn the fabric so that the seams are inside.

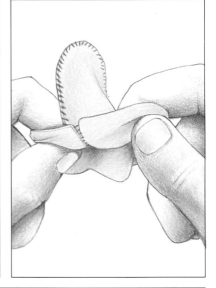

7. Stick or sew on collage materials to make the face and hair.

Variations

Sock mouth puppets

What you need:

- old sock
- fabric scraps
- sewing needle
- cotton thread
- collage materials
  (wool, beads, synthetic fur)
- scissors
- glue

Instructions:

1. Turn the sock inside out. Make a small ball (approx. 6 cm x 4 cm) with the fabric scraps.

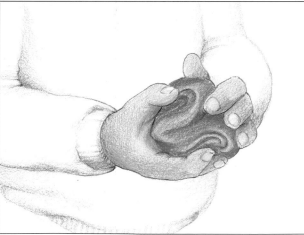

2. Firmly stitch the ball into the heel of the sock. This will make the head of the puppet.

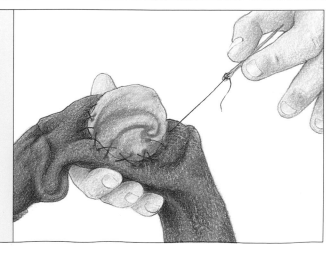

3. Turn the sock right side out and put it on your hand. Push in the toe of the sock to create the mouth.

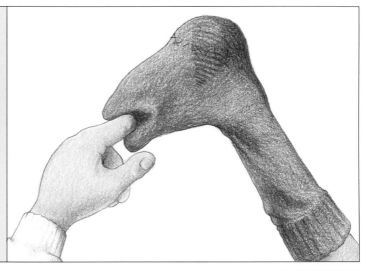

4. Stitch around the edge of the mouth to keep it in place.

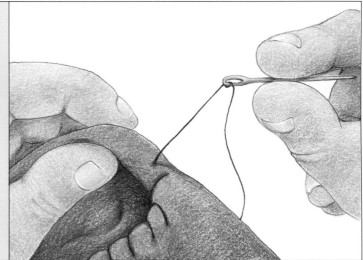

5. Add the finishing touches, e.g. hair, eyes, ears, tongue, tail, etc., using the collage materials.

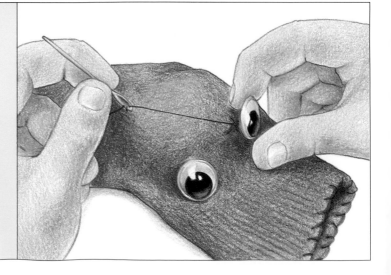

Variations

Leave out the ball of fabric in the heel.

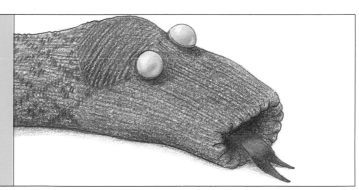

Leave the mouth unstitched.

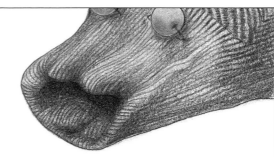

Cut out the toe of the sock. Stitch or glue in cardboard semi-circles to make the mouth.

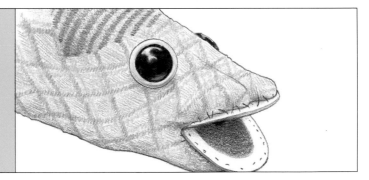

Add cardboard and foam shapes to make different characters.

Paper-plate mouth puppets

What you need:

- 2 paper plates
- stapler and staples
- scissors
- collage materials
  (felt, synthetic fur, wool)
- paint
- egg carton

Instructions:

1. Fold one paper plate in half.

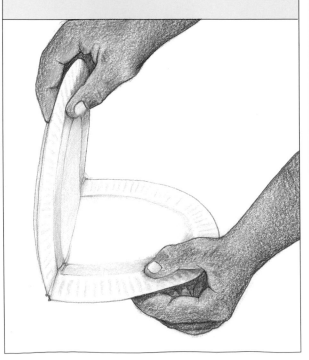

2. Cut another paper plate in half.

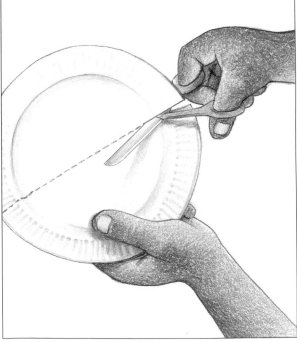

3. Staple the halves to each side of the folded plate.

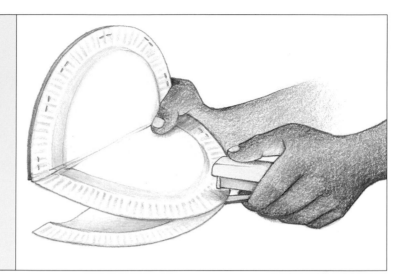

4. Glue on pieces of an egg carton for eyes.

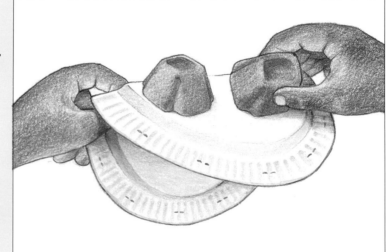

5. Add collage materials to make the character.

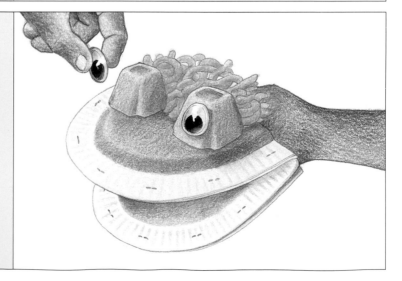

Foam mouth puppets

Instructions:

1. Cut out two pieces of foam as shown in the diagram. One piece will be slightly larger.

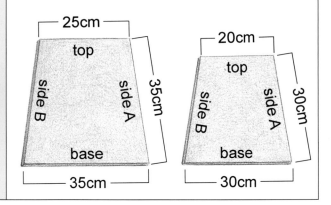

2. Take the large piece and bring the edges A and B together to form a cone shape.

3. Glue the edges together.

4. Pinch the top edge together and glue.

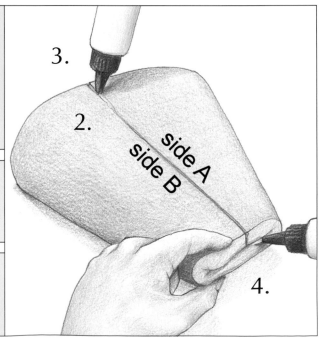

14

5. Push the top edge into the cone shape to form the mouth.

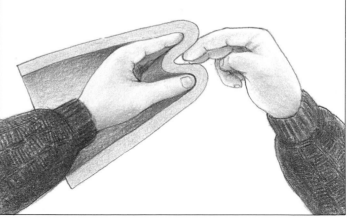

6. Repeat steps 2.—4. with the small piece of foam.

7. Glue the base edge of the small cone shape onto the top surface of the large cone shape.

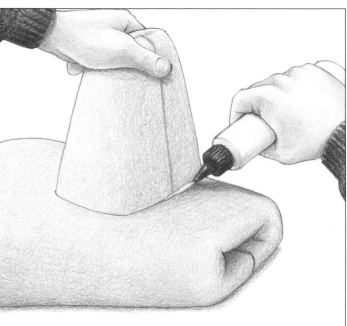

8. Push in the top edge to form the puppet's head.

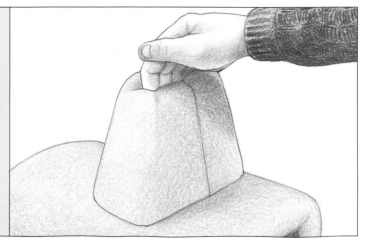

9. Make the eyes and ears with the left-over foam. Glue in place.

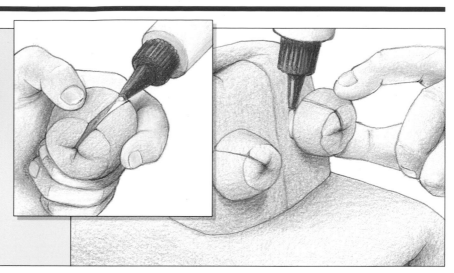

10. Complete the puppet by adding collage materials, e.g., hair, glasses, moustache, hat, etc.

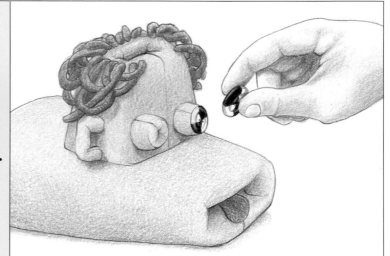

Variation

Cut out one piece of foam only. Then repeat steps 2.—5. Decorate by glueing on bits of foam as eyes, arms, legs, etc.

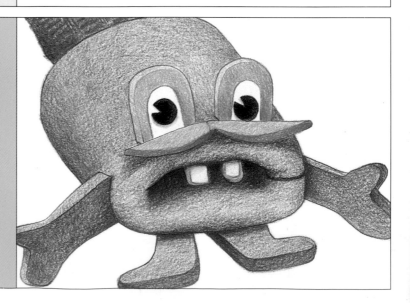

Fabric hand puppets

What you need:
- a piece of fabric (approx. 60 cm x 40 cm)
- sewing needle
- cotton thread
- scissors
- collage materials (sequins, wool, lace)
- craft glue
- paper
- pins

Instructions:

1. Photocopy the pattern on page 32 and cut it out.

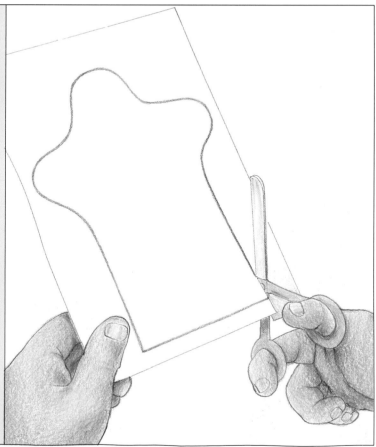

2. Fold the fabric in half. Place the pattern on the folded fabric. Trace a line around the paper pattern.

3. Cut out the two layers of fabric.

4. Decorate one piece of fabric by sewing or glueing on hair, eyes, clothes, etc.

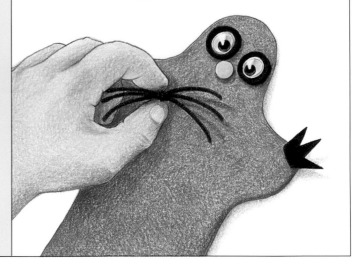

5. Put the two pieces of fabric together and sew around the edge. Leave the base edge free for your hand.

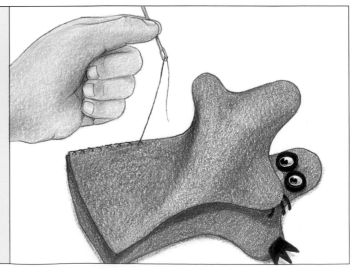

6. Turn the puppet right side out through the opening.

Variations

Use a mitten.

Use a glove.

Stick puppets

What you need:

- 1 piece of dowel (approx. 30 cm long)
- 1 satay stick (approx. 30 cm long)
- 1 polystyrene sphere
- collage materials
- paint
- string
- felt fabric
- needle and cotton thread

Instructions:

1. Paint the sphere.

2. Make the face using the collage materials.

3. Push the piece of dowel part way into the sphere.

4. Make a 1cm slit in the middle of the felt fabric.

5. Insert the dowel through the slit.

6. Gather the fabric at the top and tie with the string.

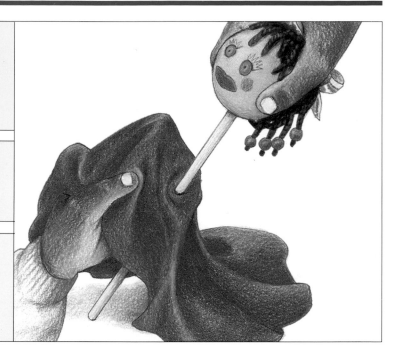

7. Cut out a hand shape from the felt fabric.

8. Stitch the hand onto the fabric about 30 cm from the puppet's head.

9. Sew a satay stick to the back of the hand.

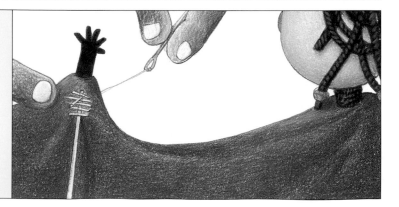

10. Use collage materials to create things the character could hold, e.g., an umbrella.

Variations

Attach two hands.

Instead of a polystyrene sphere, stuff stockings with newspaper and cover with fabric.

Shadow puppets

What you need:

- thin, stiff cardboard (24 cm x 24 cm)
- satay sticks
- pencil
- scissors
- masking tape
- overhead transparency sheets (OHT)

Instructions:

1. Draw a butterfly shape onto the cardboard.

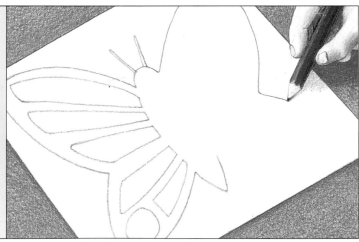

2. Cut out the shape.

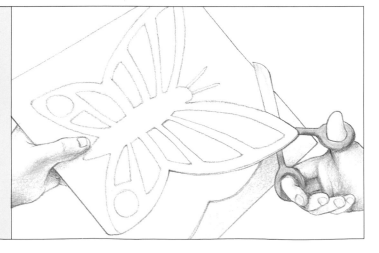

3. Cut out sections inside the shape. Tape an OHT over each section.

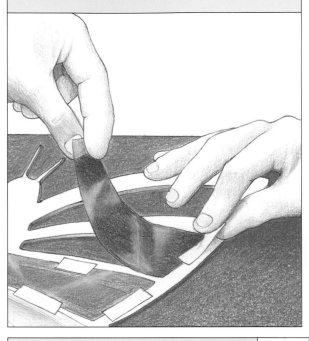

4. Tape a stick to the puppet.

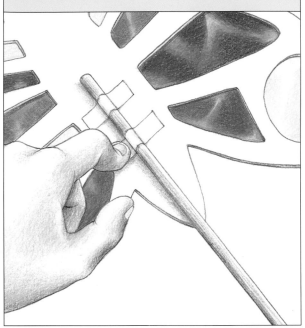

5. Manipulate the stick to make the puppet move.

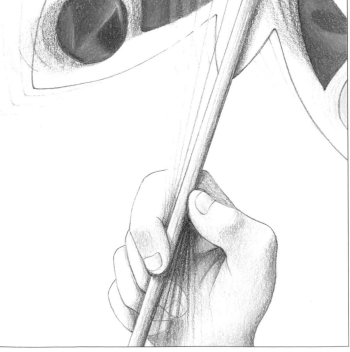

Variations

Use a felt pen to add patterns to the OHT.

Make puppets with parts that move.

Make hand shadow puppets with small paper shapes.

A shadow puppet theatre

What you need:

- a large cardboard box
- a piece of white fabric or paper the size of the screen
- a small table
- a large piece of dark fabric to cover the table
- a light source (lamp, spotlight, overhead projector)
- scissors
- paint

Instructions:

1. Cut away the back section of the box.

2. Draw a line marking the required screen size on the front.

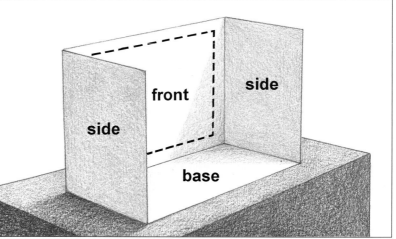

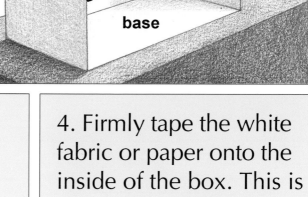

3. Cut along the line to make a space for the screen.

4. Firmly tape the white fabric or paper onto the inside of the box. This is the screen. Paint and decorate the theatre.

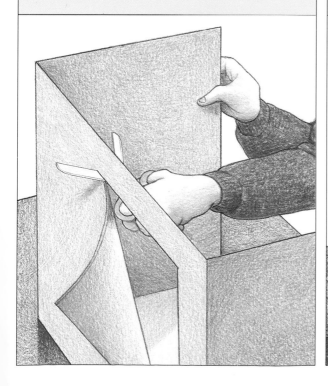

5. Position the light source so that it shines onto the screen from behind.

6. Cover the table with dark fabric
to hide the puppeteer from the audience.

Glossary

collage a picture made by pasting pieces of paper, cloth or other materials onto paper or board.

dowel a round, wooden stick or rod.

fabric cloth.

felt a non-woven cloth, which does not fray when cut.

foam a soft, springy material made by putting gas bubbles into rubber or plastic.

manipulate to make something move or act. A puppeteer manipulates a puppet's legs to make it walk.

polystyrene hard foam often used in packaging.

puppeteer a person who works a puppet.

satay stick thin, round, bamboo stick or wooden skewer used in Asian cooking.

synthetic material that does not occur naturally and is made by humans with machines, e.g., plastic.

Conversion chart * Imperial measures approximate only

1 cm	0.4 inch	20 cm	8.0 inches
2 cm	0.8 inch	24 cm	9.5 inches
4 cm	1.5 inches	25 cm	10.0 inches
6 cm	2.5 inches	30 cm	12.0 inches
8 cm	3.0 inches	35 cm	14.0 inches
10 cm	4.0 inches	40 cm	16.0 inches
14 cm	5.5 inches	60 cm	24.0 inches
15 cm	6.0 inches	80 cm	32.0 inches

Paper finger puppet pattern

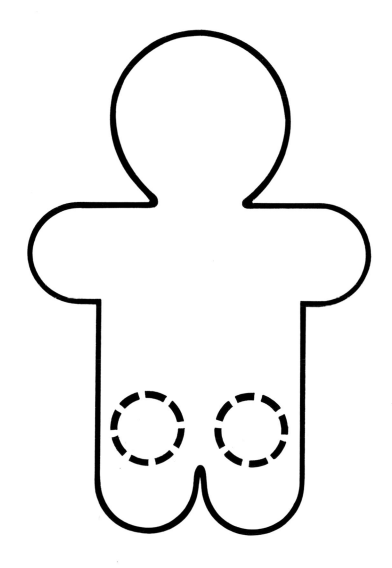

Fabric hand puppet pattern

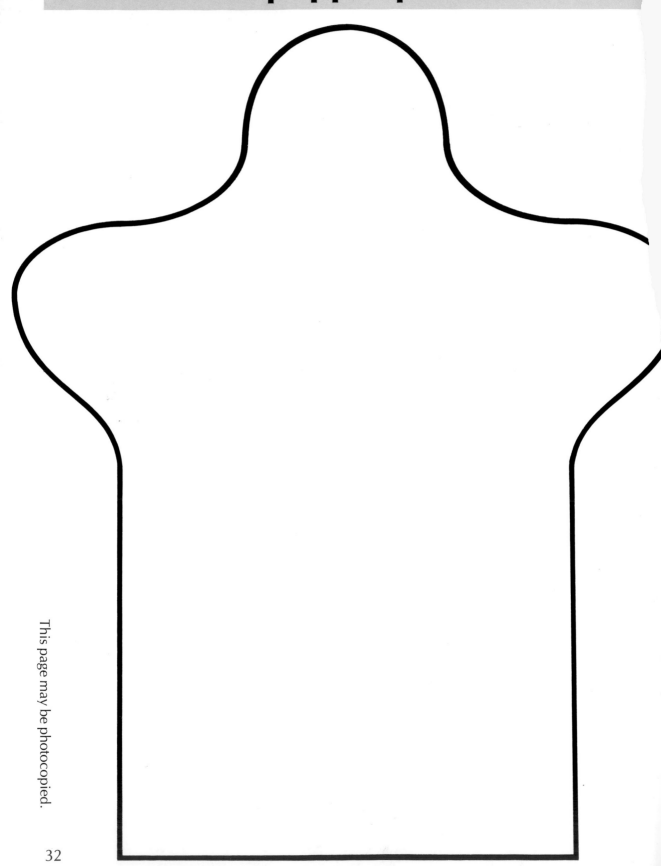